Mahabharata: Tales in Verse

Echoes of Honor, Betrayal, and Destiny

Dr. Ankush Mahajan

Dr. Shiva Durga

Copyright © <2024> Dr. Ankush Mahajan & Dr. Shiva Durga

Dedicated to the loving lotus feet: Krishna

I am the origin of all creation. Everything proceeds from Me. The wise who know this perfectly worship Me with great faith and devotion.

(Bhagavad Gita 10.8)

Contents

CONTENTS

Foreword

"Mahabharata: Tales in Verse" is a collaborative masterpiece by two distinguished scholars, Dr. Ankush Mahajan and Dr. Shiva Durga, offering a poetic exploration of the ancient Indian epic, the Mahabharata. Through their combined efforts, this collection presents the profound narratives, characters, and teachings of the epic in a new and captivating light, resonating with readers of all backgrounds.

At the core of the Mahabharata lies the enigmatic figure of Lord Krishna, who serves as the charioteer to the Pandava prince, Arjuna, and imparts the divine teachings of the Bhagavad Gita. In their poems dedicated to Krishna, the authors unveil his multifaceted nature – the playful cowherd, the compassionate friend, the astute strategist, and the embodiment of divinity – offering profound insights into duty, righteousness, and the human condition.

Alongside Krishna, the poems bring to life a myriad of characters, each with their own compelling stories and moral dilemmas. From Arjuna, torn between familial loyalty and his duty as a warrior, to Yudhishthira, the righteous eldest Pandava facing tests of truth and honor, and Bhima, the mighty warrior driven by justice, each character represents a different facet of the human experience.

Through their poems, Dr. Mahajan and Dr. Durga delve into the innermost thoughts, emotions, and struggles of these characters, shedding light on the complexities of human nature and the choices we face in life. They invite readers to rediscover the timeless wisdom of the Mahabharata and to find inspiration in its profound teachings on courage, compassion, loyalty, and righteousness.

"Mahabharata: Tales in Verse" is not just a retelling of an ancient epic; it is a reflection of our own lives, with its triumphs and tragedies, its joys and sorrows. It is a testament to the enduring power of storytelling and its ability to illuminate the human experience. As you embark on this poetic journey, may you find in these verses the same courage, compassion, and insight that have guided countless generations through the timeless tale of the Mahabharata.

Preface

The Mahabharata, an ancient Indian epic, is a monumental work that has fascinated and inspired countless generations. Its profound narratives, intricate characters, and timeless teachings continue to resonate with readers across the globe. In "Mahabharata: Tales in Verse," we, Dr. Ankush Mahajan and Dr. Shiva Durga, seek to bring this epic to life in a new and poetic form, offering fresh perspectives on its eternal truths and wisdom.

Our journey into the Mahabharata has been one of deep reverence and introspection. As scholars and writers, we have always been captivated by the richness of its stories and the complexity of its characters. This book is our attempt to distill the essence of the Mahabharata through the medium of poetry, making it accessible and engaging to modern readers.

At the heart of this epic is the enigmatic figure of Lord Krishna, whose divine teachings in the Bhagavad Gita provide profound insights into the nature of duty, righteousness, and the human condition. His guidance to Arjuna on the battlefield of Kurukshetra transcends time, offering wisdom that is as relevant today as it was thousands of years ago. In our poems dedicated to

Krishna, we explore his multifaceted nature – from the playful cowherd to the compassionate friend, the astute strategist, and the embodiment of divinity.

The Mahabharata is populated with a myriad of characters, each facing their own moral dilemmas and struggles. Through our verses, we delve into the innermost thoughts and emotions of these characters, shedding light on the complexities of human nature. From Arjuna's internal conflict and Yudhishthira's pursuit of truth to Draupadi's unwavering resilience and Karna's tragic loyalty, each poem seeks to capture the essence of these timeless figures.

Our poetic exploration goes beyond mere retellings of the epic's stories. We aim to offer new insights and interpretations, inviting readers to reflect on the moral and philosophical dimensions of the Mahabharata. The themes of honor, betrayal, duty, and destiny are universal, resonating with readers of all ages and backgrounds.

In writing this book, we have been guided by a desire to bridge the past and the present, to make the ancient wisdom of the Mahabharata accessible to contemporary audiences. Whether you are a scholar of Indian mythology, a spiritual seeker, or simply a lover of literature, we hope that "Mahabharata: Tales in Verse" will captivate, inspire, and enlighten you.

We extend our gratitude to all those who have supported us in this endeavor. It is our sincere hope that this collection of poems will serve as a source of reflection and inspiration, encouraging readers to explore the depths of their own experiences and the world around them.

In conclusion, "Mahabharata: Tales in Verse" is not just a book; it is an invitation to embark on a poetic journey through one of the greatest epics of all time. We are honored to share this journey with you and look forward to the conversations and insights it will inspire.

Dr. Ankush Mahajan & Dr. Shiva Durga

Acknowledgments

Writing "Mahabharata: Tales in Verse" has been an extraordinary journey, and we are deeply grateful to those who have supported us along the way. This book would not have been possible without the encouragement, guidance, and love of many individuals and institutions.

First and foremost, we express our heartfelt gratitude to our families, whose unwavering support and understanding have been the bedrock of our efforts. Your patience and belief in us have been our greatest sources of strength.

We extend our sincere thanks to our friends and colleagues who have provided invaluable feedback and encouragement throughout this project. Your insights and suggestions have enriched our work in countless ways.

We are profoundly grateful to the scholars and researchers whose studies on the Mahabharata have illuminated our path. Your work has been an inspiration and a guiding light, helping us to delve deeper into the epic's intricate narratives and timeless wisdom.

Special thanks go to our publishers, who believed in our vision and provided the platform to bring this book to life. Your support and professional expertise have been instrumental in shaping this work.

We are also indebted to the readers and lovers of literature who have shared their enthusiasm and passion for the Mahabharata. Your interest in this epic has motivated us to explore its depths and present it in a poetic form that is both accessible and engaging.

To the divine inspiration of Lord Krishna and the timeless characters of the Mahabharata, we owe a debt of gratitude. Your stories and teachings continue to guide and inspire us, offering profound insights into the nature of life, duty, and the human condition.

Lastly, we thank each other for the collaborative spirit and dedication that have been the hallmark of our partnership. This book is a testament to our shared vision and our love for the Mahabharata.

With deep appreciation,

Dr. Ankush Mahajan & Dr. Shiva Durga

Prologue/Introduction

In the timeless epic of the Mahabharata, lies a tapestry of narratives, woven with threads of honor, betrayal, and destiny. It is a saga of profound wisdom, profound emotions, and profound dilemmas. At its heart beats the enigmatic figure of Krishna, the divine charioteer, the philosopher, the guide, and the friend. "Mahabharata: Tales in Verse" invites you to immerse yourself in this epic world through the lens of poetry, where each character, each event, and each emotion is painted with the strokes of rhythm and rhyme.

As we embark on this poetic journey, we are introduced to Krishna, not merely as a character but as the very essence of the epic. His presence is felt in every verse, guiding the destinies of mortals, shaping the course of battles, and imparting timeless wisdom that resonates through the ages. Through the verses dedicated to Krishna, we witness his multifaceted persona – the mischievous cowherd of Vrindavan, the astute strategist of the Kurukshetra battlefield, the compassionate counselor to kings, and above all, the divine being whose actions transcend human understanding.

Alongside Krishna, we encounter a myriad of characters, each with their own tales of valor, sacrifice, and tragedy. Arjuna, the mighty warrior conflicted by duty and compassion; Draupadi, the fiery queen whose resilience is unmatched; Yudhishthira, the epitome of righteousness facing moral dilemmas; Bhima, whose strength is equaled only by his heart; Nakula and Sahadeva, the twins whose skills complement their brothers' prowess; Duryodhana, the ambitious prince consumed by envy and pride; Dushasana, the pawn in his brother's schemes; Karna, the tragic hero bound by loyalty and fate; Bhishma, the venerable grandsire torn between duty and love; Drona and Kripacharya, the noble teachers caught in the web of politics and war; Vidura, the wise counselor whose words echo truth; Dhritarashtra, the blind king whose love for his sons blinds his judgment; Gandhari, the devoted wife whose sacrifice knows no bounds; Sanjaya, the narrator blessed with divine sight; and countless others whose lives intertwine in the grand tapestry of the Mahabharata.

Through the poems dedicated to each character, we delve deep into their psyche, unraveling their motivations, fears, and desires. We witness their triumphs and failures, their joys and sorrows, their loves and losses. We see ourselves reflected in their struggles, for the Mahabharata is not just a story of ancient heroes but a mirror to our own lives, with its eternal themes of duty, loyalty, betrayal, and redemption.

As we turn the pages of "Mahabharata: Tales in Verse," we are reminded that the epic is not just a relic of the past but a living, breathing narrative that continues to resonate with relevance in today's world. Its lessons are timeless, its characters are immortal, and its wisdom is infinite. Through poetry, we hope to rekindle the flame of this ancient epic, to make it accessible to a new generation of readers, to inspire them to seek truth, to uphold righteousness, and to embrace their own destinies with courage and grace.

Join us on this poetic odyssey through the Mahabharata, where every verse is a testament to the enduring power of storytelling, where every character is a beacon of light in the darkness of ignorance, and where every tale is a reminder of our shared humanity. "Mahabharata: Tales in Verse" awaits you, dear reader, to embark on a journey of discovery, enlightenment, and above all, a journey of the soul.

Section - 1

1. Characters of the Mahabharata: A Poetic Tribute

1.1. Krishna: The Divine Maestro

In the annals of time, where echoes resound,
A tale of honor and destiny, in verses profound.
Mahabharata's saga, in Krishna's light,
A divine maestro, in the epic's flight.

Born of Devaki, amidst darkness and woe,
To Vasudeva's care, his parents did bestow.
In Gokul's embrace, his childhood did bloom,
A playful deity, dispelling all gloom.

As the charioteer to Arjuna, he did stand,
On Kurukshetra's field, guiding with a divine hand.
The Bhagavad Gita, his wisdom did impart,
Echoes of honor and duty, to every heart.

In Draupadi's anguish, he did intervene,
Clothing her in endless sarees, unseen.
A symbol of protection, in times of despair,
His presence, a solace, beyond compare.

In the game of dice, he played his part,
As a messenger of peace, to Duryodhana's heart.
Yet, the dice of fate, were cast in strife,
Leading to years of exile and life's endless rife.

In the war of Kurukshetra, his strategy shone,
A master tactician, his plans were drawn.

From the Sudarshana Chakra, to his divine form,
Krishna's presence, a beacon in the storm.

In the end, as the Yadavas met their fate,
Through fratricidal strife, sealing their state.
Krishna's departure, a poignant decree,
Marking the end, of an era's spree.

In echoes of honor, betrayal's stark,
Krishna's role, a divine lark.
In Mahabharata's tale, his legend sings,
A timeless saga, on destiny's wings.

Thus, in tales of yore, Krishna's name,
Echoes of honor, in destiny's game.
A divine maestro, in life's grand verse,
Mahabharata's soul, in Krishna's hearse.

1.2. Arjuna: The Archer's Ode

In Hastinapura's realm, a prince so fair,
Arjuna, with Gandiva, beyond compare.
A warrior skilled, in archery's art,
In Kurukshetra's war, he'd play his part.

Son of Kunti, and the wind god too,
His prowess in battle, none could subdue.
With eyes set on the target, steady and clear,
Arjuna, the mighty, without fear.

In the Pandava clan, he stood tall,
With Bhima, Nakula, and Sahadeva, answering the call.
Yudhishthira's charioteer, in life's grand race,
Arjuna, the warrior, in every case.

On Kurukshetra's field, the battle's roar,
Arjuna, with Krishna, his charioteer, in the war.
The Bhagavad Gita, his heart did heed,
Guiding him through doubt and creed.

In Draupadi's swayamvara, he won her hand,
A test of skill, in a noble stand.
His love for Subhadra, a tale of yore,
Arjuna, the lover, forevermore.

With Karna, his rivalry, deep and fierce,
In battle, their clash, the world did pierce.

Yet, in respect and honor, Arjuna did see,
A warrior noble, in destiny's decree.

In exile, he wandered, in search of truth,
Arjuna, the seeker, in age and youth.
His penance and prayers, to the heavens above,
Seeking guidance, in virtue and love.

In the end, his legacy, a tale of old,
Arjuna's valor, in tales untold.
A hero of honor, in destiny's flight,
Arjuna, the archer, in eternal light.

Thus, in echoes of honor, betrayal's tale,
Arjuna's saga, in verses pale.
A warrior's ode, in destiny's rhyme,
Arjuna's legacy, in the sands of time.

1.3. Yudhishthira: The Paragon of Virtue

In the lineage of Bharata, a prince so fair,
Yudhishthira, with virtues rare.
Known for his righteousness, his dharma untold,
In the annals of time, his story unfolds.

Eldest of the Pandavas, a king in his own right,
Yudhishthira's valor, in honor's light.
His word was his bond, his truth unshakeable,
In the game of life, he was unbreakable.

In the court of Kuru, a game of dice,
Yudhishthira's kingdom, paid the price.
Yet, in exile, his honor he'd keep,
In virtue and truth, he'd forever leap.

As a charioteer to Krishna, he'd ride,
In the battle of Kurukshetra, with destiny's tide.
His wisdom and counsel, in every choice,
Yudhishthira, the king, in every voice.

In the end, his ascent to heaven's gate,
Yudhishthira's virtue, in timeless state.
A paragon of righteousness, in life's grandeur,
Yudhishthira's legacy, forever pure.

Thus, in echoes of honor, his story prevails,

Yudhishthira's virtue, in every tale.
A king of kings, in dharma's embrace,
Yudhishthira's spirit, in eternal grace.

1.4. Bhima: The Titan's Heart

In the land of Kuru, a warrior stood,
Bhima, with muscles like ironwood.
A titan of strength, with a lion's roar,
In the epic's tale, his valor did soar.

Second of the Pandavas, mighty and bold,
Bhima's story, in battles untold.
With a mace in hand, he'd strike the foe,
A warrior fierce, in every blow.

In the forests of exile, his deeds did shine,
Bhima, the protector, in every line.
From demons to giants, he'd conquer all,
In the Pandava's quest, he'd stand tall.

In the game of dice, his anger did rise,
Bhima's oath, a solemn guise.
To slay Duryodhana, his sworn foe,
In Kurukshetra's field, his wrath did show.

As a brother, loyal and true,
Bhima's love, forever grew.
With Yudhishthira's word, he'd comply,
In duty and honor, he'd never shy.

In the end, his ascent to the heavens above,
Bhima's strength, a tale of love.
A warrior of might, in every part,
Bhima, the titan, with a lion's heart.

Thus, in echoes of honor, his saga does last,
Bhima's valor, in memories vast.
A hero of heroes, in the epic's retold,
Bhima's legacy, in legends bold.

1.5. Nakula: The Graceful Swordsman

You In the land of Kurus, a prince so fair,
Nakula, with grace beyond compare.
A swordsman skilled, with a heart so pure,
In the Pandava's tale, his valor secure.

Twin to Sahadeva, in virtue aligned,
Nakula's presence, forever enshrined.
With a sword in hand, he'd wield with grace,
A warrior noble, in every space.

In the forests of exile, his skills did shine,
Nakula, the hunter, in every line.
With bow and arrow, he'd hit his mark,
A master of weapons, in light and dark.

In the game of dice, his honor he'd hold,
Nakula's loyalty, a tale of old.
To his brothers, he'd stand with pride,
In duty and honor, he'd never hide.

In the war of Kurukshetra, his role defined,
Nakula, the warrior, with valor refined.
His courage and strength, in every fight,
A hero of grace, in honor's light.

In the end, his journey to the heavens above,
Nakula's legacy, a tale of love.
A warrior of grace, in every part,
Nakula, the swordsman, with a noble heart.

Thus, in echoes of honor, his story is told,
Nakula's valor, in verses bold.
A hero of virtue, in the epic's retold,
Nakula's legacy, in legends of old.

1.6. Sahadeva: The Wise Twin

In the kingdom of Kuru, a prince so wise,
Sahadeva, with knowledge that flies.
A twin to Nakula, in grace and might,
In the Pandava's saga, his wisdom takes flight.

With numbers and strategy, he'd always excel,
Sahadeva's intellect, a story to tell.
In the game of dice, his foresight was keen,
A master of tactics, in every scene.

In the forests of exile, his skills did bloom,
Sahadeva, the hunter, in nature's room.
With bow and arrow, he'd hit the mark,
A warrior skilled, in light and dark.

In the war of Kurukshetra, his presence shone,
Sahadeva, the commander, with courage grown.
His plans and strategies, in every fight,
A hero of wisdom, in honor's light.

In the end, his journey to the celestial abode,
Sahadeva's legacy, a tale of the road.
A warrior of wisdom, in every part,
Sahadeva, the wise twin, with a noble heart.

Thus, in echoes of honor, his story does dwell,
Sahadeva's valor, in verses that swell.
A hero of intellect, in the epic's grand shell,
Sahadeva's legacy, in legends that tell.

1.7. Draupadi: The Flame of Courage

In the halls of Panchala, a princess born,
Draupadi, radiant as the morn.
Of beauty unmatched, and fire within,
Her tale of courage, a saga to begin.

Born of fire, a maiden of grace,
Draupadi, with destiny, embraced.
Wife to five, yet a queen in her own right,
Her honor and valor, a guiding light.

In the court of Kuru, a dice's cruel play,
Draupadi, in shame, they sought to sway.
Her dignity, her pride, she held dear,
In the face of adversity, without fear.

In Hastinapura's halls, her voice did rise,
Challenging the norms, with fiery eyes.
Injustice she fought, with words so bold,
Draupadi, a heroine, of stories old.

In the exile's hardships, she bore her share,
Draupadi, with strength beyond compare.
Her wisdom, her wit, in every test,
A queen of hearts, in the Pandava's quest.

In Kurukshetra's field, her role defined,
Draupadi, the beacon, of a warrior's kind.
Her words, her actions, in battle's cry,

A symbol of strength, that reached the sky.

In the end, her sacrifice, a tale of grace,
Draupadi's valor, in every trace.
A heroine's saga, in honor's flame,
Draupadi's legacy, forever the same.

Thus, in echoes of honor, her story told,
Draupadi's courage, in verses bold.
A queen of hearts, in destiny's play,
Draupadi's spirit, forever to stay.

1.8. Duryodhana: The Ambitious Prince

In the court of Kuru, a prince did rise,
Duryodhana, with ambition's eyes.
A son of Dhritarashtra, with a heart of stone,
In the epic's tale, his legacy is known.

Eldest of the Kauravas, proud and bold,
Duryodhana's story, in ambition's hold.
With jealousy and rage, his path was paved,
A prince of power, in honor's grave.

In the game of dice, his greed did show,
Duryodhana's downfall, in ambition's glow.
His rivalry with the Pandavas, deep and fierce,
In battle, their clash, the world did pierce.

As a king, he ruled with an iron hand,
Injustice and pride, his kingdom did stand.
Yet, in loyalty to his brothers, he'd never sway,
In duty and honor, he'd always stay.

In the war of Kurukshetra, his fate was sealed,
Duryodhana's downfall, in destiny's field.
His end, a tragic tale of pride's fall,
A prince of ambition, standing tall.

In the end, his legacy, a cautionary tale,
Duryodhana's ambition, in pride's frail.
A prince of power, in ambition's trance,

Duryodhana's legacy, in destiny's dance.

Thus, in echoes of honor, his story is told,
Duryodhana's ambition, in verses bold.
A prince of pride, in the epic's grand fold,
Duryodhana's legacy, in ambition's hold.

1.9. Dushasana: The Shadow of Vice

In the halls of Hastinapura, a prince so dark,
Dushasana, with shadows that stark.
A shadow of vice, in the Kuru clan,
In the epic's tale, his infamy began.

Brother to Duryodhana, in sin aligned,
Dushasana's deeds, forever enshrined.
With malice in heart, he'd cause great woe,
A villainous figure, in every blow.

In the court of Kuru, his cruelty did reign,
Dushasana's malice, a mark of disdain.
In Draupadi's swayamvara, he'd show his might,
In dishonor and shame, he'd take delight.

In the game of dice, his actions did speak,
Dushasana's treachery, in actions bleak.
To disrobe Draupadi, his heinous sin,
In the epic's tale, his downfall did begin.

In the war of Kurukshetra, his fate was sealed,
Dushasana's end, in battle revealed.
A villain of vice, in every part,
Dushasana, the shadow, with a darkened heart.

Thus, in echoes of dishonor, his story is told,
Dushasana's villainy, in verses bold.
A figure of sin, in the epic's retold,

Dushasana's legacy, in darkness cold.

19

1.10. Karna: The Son of the Sun

In the kingdom of Kuru, a warrior born,
Karna, with destiny's horn.
Son of Kunti, yet the sun god's heir,
In the epic's tale, his valor rare.

With armor and earrings, radiant and bright,
Karna's prowess, in valor's light.
A warrior unmatched, in skill and might,
In every battle, his strength took flight.

In Hastinapura's court, he stood tall,
Karna's honor, never to fall.
In friendship and loyalty, he'd forever bind,
A true friend, in heart and mind.

In the game of dice, his fate was sealed,
Karna's honor, never to yield.
To his word and duty, he'd forever stand,
A warrior noble, in every land.

In the war of Kurukshetra, his prowess shone,
Karna, with bow, his enemies he'd disown.
His valor and courage, in every fight,
A hero of honor, in honor's light.

In the end, his fate, a tragic end,
Karna's legacy, a tale to mend.
A warrior of valor, in every part,
Karna, the son of the sun, with a noble heart.

Thus, in echoes of honor, his story's sung,
Karna's valor, in every tongue.
A hero of the epic, in battles strung,
Karna's legacy, in the heavens hung.

1.11. Bhishma: The Grand Patriarch

In the land of Bharat, a noble soul,
Bhishma, with virtues that control.
A patriarch grand, with a heart so pure,
In the Mahabharata, his legacy secure.

Son of Ganga, and the king of kings,
Bhishma's wisdom, in every thing.
A vow of celibacy, he'd faithfully keep,
In duty and honor, he'd forever leap.

As a warrior unmatched, in prowess and might,
Bhishma's valor, in every fight.
With the boon of choosing his death's hour,
Bhishma's resolve, a testament of power.

In the court of Hastinapura, his word was law,
Bhishma's counsel, without a flaw.
A protector of the Kuru clan's throne,
In every challenge, he'd stand alone.

In the war of Kurukshetra, his loyalty showed,
Bhishma, with bow, his enemies he'd goad.
His sacrifice and valor, in every fight,
A hero of honor, in honor's light.

In the end, his vow, a solemn decree,
Bhishma's legacy, in eternity.
A warrior of virtue, in every part,

Bhishma, the grand patriarch, in every heart.

Thus, in echoes of honor, his story's told,
Bhishma's valor, in verses bold.
A hero of the epic, in battles cold,
Bhishma's legacy, in legends of old.

1.12. Drona: The Master of Warfare

In the land of Kurukshetra, a teacher renowned,
Drona, with wisdom that astound.
A master of warfare, with skills so rare,
In the epic's saga, his presence flare.

As a teacher of princes, he'd impart,
Drona's knowledge, a priceless art.
In archery and combat, he'd excel,
A guru supreme, in every spell.

In the Kuru court, his loyalty shown,
Drona's counsel, a wisdom sown.
A friend to the Pandavas, yet duty bound,
In every challenge, his honor sound.

In the war of Kurukshetra, his role defined,
Drona, the commander, with strategy lined.
His valor and courage, in every fight,
A hero of honor, in honor's light.

In the end, his fate, a tragic end,
Drona's legacy, a tale to mend.
A warrior of skill, in every part,
Drona, the master, with a noble heart.

Thus, in echoes of honor, his story's sung,
Drona's valor, in every tongue.
A hero of the epic, in battles strung,

Drona's legacy, in the heavens hung.

25

1.13. Kripacharya: The Sage Warrior

In the realm of Kurukshetra, a sage did stand,
Kripacharya, with wisdom so grand.
A warrior and teacher, with virtues rare,
In the Mahabharata, his legacy fair.

A mentor to princes, he'd guide with grace,
Kripacharya's wisdom, a divine trace.
In the arts of warfare, he'd excel,
A guru supreme, in every spell.

In the court of Hastinapura, his counsel wise,
Kripacharya's loyalty, a noble prize.
A friend to the Pandavas, in every plight,
In duty and honor, he'd shine bright.

In the war of Kurukshetra, his valor known,
Kripacharya, with bow, his enemies he'd disown.
His courage and strength, in every fight,
A hero of honor, in honor's light.

In the end, his legacy, a tale of old,
Kripacharya's valor, in verses bold.
A warrior sage, in every part,
Kripacharya, the sage warrior, with a noble heart.

Thus, in echoes of honor, his story's sung,
Kripacharya's valor, in every tongue.
A hero of the epic, in battles strung,

Kripacharya's legacy, forever young.

27

1.14. Vidura: The Voice of Wisdom

In the court of Kurus, a voice so wise,
Vidura, with wisdom that flies.
A counselor true, with a heart so pure,
In the Mahabharata, his words endure.

Son of Vyas and a royal maid,
Vidura's wisdom, in every shade.
A voice of reason, in times of strife,
In every challenge, he'd seek life.

In the halls of Hastinapura, his counsel strong,
Vidura's guidance, a lifelong song.
A friend to the Pandavas, in every need,
In every counsel, his wisdom feed.

In the game of dice, his truth did shine,
Vidura's honor, a noble line.
To his word and duty, he'd forever stand,
A voice of truth, in every land.

In the war of Kurukshetra, his wisdom shown,
Vidura, the advisor, with knowledge grown.
His foresight and counsel, in every fight,
A hero of wisdom, in honor's light.

In the end, his journey to the forest deep,
Vidura's legacy, a tale to keep.
A sage of virtue, in every part,
Vidura, the voice of wisdom, with a noble heart.

Thus, in echoes of honor, his story's told,
Vidura's wisdom, in verses bold.
A hero of the epic, in wisdom's fold,
Vidura's legacy, in legends old.

1.15. Dhritarashtra: The Blind King

In the land of Kurus, a king so grand,
Dhritarashtra, with fate in hand.
Blind from birth, yet a ruler bold,
In the Mahabharata, his story told.

Father of a hundred sons, he'd reign,
Dhritarashtra's kingdom, in joy and pain.
A father torn, between love and pride,
In every choice, he'd confide.

In the halls of Hastinapura, his word was law,
Dhritarashtra's reign, without a flaw.
In the game of dice, his kingdom's fate,
In every challenge, he'd contemplate.

In the war of Kurukshetra, his heart did weep,
Dhritarashtra's sorrow, in memories deep.
His sons' demise, a tragic toll,
In every loss, he'd console.

In the end, his kingdom lost,
Dhritarashtra's fate, a heavy cost.
A king of sorrow, in every part,
Dhritarashtra, the blind king, with a heavy heart.

Thus, in echoes of honor, his story's sung,
Dhritarashtra's reign, in verses hung.
A king of kings, in sorrow's tongue,
Dhritarashtra's legacy, in the songs of young.

1.16. Gandhari: The Virtuous Queen

In the halls of Hastinapura, a queen did reside,
Gandhari, with virtues that abide.
Wife to Dhritarashtra, the blind king,
In the Mahabharata, her praises ring.

Blindfolded in devotion, to share her husband's fate,
Gandhari's sacrifice, a story great.
A mother of a hundred sons, she'd bear,
In every joy and every care.

In the court of Kurus, her voice was strong,
Gandhari's wisdom, in every song.
A mother torn, between love and fear,
In every loss, she'd shed a tear.

In the war of Kurukshetra, her heart did break,
Gandhari's sorrow, in every ache.
Her sons' demise, a heavy toll,
In every grief, she'd console.

In the end, her kingdom lost,
Gandhari's fate, a heavy cost.
A queen of virtue, in every part,
Gandhari, the virtuous queen, with a noble heart.

Thus, in echoes of honor, her story's sung,
Gandhari's sacrifice, in verses hung.

A queen of queens, in sorrow's tongue,
Gandhari's legacy, in the songs of young.

1.17. Shakuni: The Master of Deceit

In the halls of Gandhara, a prince did dwell,
Shakuni, with schemes that swell.
A master of deceit, with a heart so cold,
In the Mahabharata, his story told.

Brother to Gandhari, with vengeance deep,
Shakuni's hatred, in secrets keep.
A mind so twisted, in every plan,
In every scheme, he'd take a stand.

In the court of Hastinapura, his plots did brew,
Shakuni's treachery, in every view.
A master manipulator, with a web so wide,
In every deceit, he'd take pride.

In the game of dice, his dice were loaded,
Shakuni's cunning, in every code.
To his nephew's ruin, he'd lead the way,
In every move, he'd betray.

In Gandhara's prince, vengeance did brew,
Against the Kurus, his hatred he drew.
A puppeteer of fate, with strings unseen,
In every move, he'd intervene.

In the war of Kurukshetra, his schemes did unfold,
Shakuni, with deceit, his enemies he'd enfold.
His tricks and traps, in every fight,

A villain of cunning, in honor's blight.

In the end, his fate, a dark descent,
Shakuni's legacy, a tale of torment.
A master of deceit, in every part,
Shakuni, the schemer, with a blackened heart.

Thus, in echoes of honor, his story's sung,
Shakuni's treachery, in verses strung.
A villain of villains, in the epic's tongue,
Shakuni's legacy, in infamy hung.

1.18. Sanjaya: The Narrator of Truth

In the court of Hastinapura, a charioteer so wise,
Sanjaya, with insight that flies.
A narrator of truth, with a heart so clear,
In the Mahabharata, his voice sincere.

Charioteer to the blind king, Dhritarashtra's guide,
Sanjaya's vision, in every stride.
A witness to the epic's tale, he'd see,
In every scene, he'd be.

In the halls of Kurus, his words were gold,
Sanjaya's narration, in stories bold.
A storyteller supreme, with a tale to tell,
In every word, he'd dwell.

In the war of Kurukshetra, his eyes did see,
Sanjaya, the seer, with insight free.
His words of wisdom, in every fight,
A narrator of truth, in honor's light.

In the end, his voice, a guide's decree,
Sanjaya's legacy, in eternity.
A narrator of truth, in every part,
Sanjaya, the seer, with a noble heart.

Thus, in echoes of honor, his story's sung,
Sanjaya's narration, in verses hung.
A storyteller of the epic, in words strung,

Sanjaya's legacy, forever young.

1.19. Kunti: The Mother of Heroes

In the land kurukshetra Kunti, a queen so fair,
Kunti, with grace beyond compare.
A mother of heroes, with a heart so true,
In the Mahabharata, her valor grew.

Daughter of Shurasena, and sister so kind,
Kunti's virtues, in every mind.
A wife to Pandu, with love so pure,
In every trial, she'd endure.

In the court of Hastinapura, her sons did shine,
Kunti's pride, in every line.
A mother of five, yet a queen in her own right,
In every challenge, she'd take flight.

In the forest of exile, her strength did show,
Kunti, the mother, in every woe.
With Draupadi and her sons, she'd face,
In every hardship, she'd embrace.

In the war of Kurukshetra, her sons did fight,
Kunti, the mother, in every plight.
Her courage and wisdom, in every fight,
A mother of heroes, in honor's light.

In the end, her legacy, a tale of old,
Kunti's love, in verses bold.
A mother of valor, in every part,
Kunti, the mother of heroes, with a noble heart.

Thus, in echoes of honor, her story's sung,
Kunti's love, in verses hung.
A mother of mothers, in the epic's retold,
Kunti's legacy, in legends bold.

1.20. Dhrishtadyumna: The Warrior Prince

In the land of Panchala, a prince did rise,
Dhrishtadyumna, with valor that skies.
A warrior born, with a heart so bold,
In the Mahabharata, his tale is told.

Son of Drupada, the king so grand,
Dhrishtadyumna's prowess, in every land.
A warrior skilled, in archery's art,
In every battle, he'd play his part.

In the court of Panchala, his voice was strong,
Dhrishtadyumna's valor, a warrior's song.
A brother to Draupadi, in every fight,
In every challenge, he'd take flight.

In the war of Kurukshetra, his role defined,
Dhrishtadyumna, the commander, with courage lined.
His leadership and strategy, in every fight,
A hero of valor, in honor's light.

In the end, his fate, a warrior's end,
Dhrishtadyumna's legacy, a tale to blend.
A warrior prince, in every part,
Dhrishtadyumna, the warrior prince, with a noble heart.

Thus, in echoes of honor, his story's sung,
Dhrishtadyumna's valor, in verses strung.
A warrior of warriors, in battles flung,

Dhrishtadyumna's legacy, in epics hung.

1.21. Vrushali: The Forgotten Queen

In the land of Anga, a queen so fair,
Vrushali, with grace beyond compare.
Wife to Karna, the noble and brave,
In the Mahabharata, her story engraved.

A queen of beauty, with a heart so pure,
Vrushali's love, forever endure.
In the court of Hastinapura, her presence rare,
In every trial, she'd show her care.

In the shadow of Karna, she'd stand,
Vrushali's strength, like a silent band.
A wife so loyal, in every role,
In every hardship, she'd console.

In the war of Kurukshetra, her heart did bleed,
Vrushali, with Karna, in every need.
Her sacrifice and love, in every fight,
A queen of valor, in honor's light.

In the end, her fate, a tragic tale,
Vrushali's legacy, in verses frail.
A queen forgotten, in history's art,
Vrushali, the silent queen, with a noble heart.

Thus, in echoes of honor, her story's sung,
Vrushali's love, in verses flung.
A queen of queens, in love's lung,

Vrushali's legacy, in silence hung.

1.22. Abhimanyu: The Young Warrior

In the land of Kurukshetra, a hero was born,
Abhimanyu, with valor adorned.
Son of Arjuna and Subhadra fair,
In the Mahabharata, his legend rare.

A prince of prowess, with a heart so bold,
Abhimanyu's story, forever told.
In the womb, he learned the art of war,
In every battle, he'd raise the bar.

In the court of Virata, his skills did show,
Abhimanyu's valor, in every blow.
A warrior skilled, beyond his years,
In every challenge, he'd face his fears.

In the Chakravyuha, his fate was cast,
Abhimanyu's courage, unsurpassed.
To break the formation, he'd strive alone,
In every turn, he'd hold his own.

In the war of Kurukshetra, his bravery shone,
Abhimanyu, with bow, his enemies he'd disown.
His valor and skill, in every fight,
A hero of youth, in honor's light.

In the end, his fate, a tragic end,
Abhimanyu's legacy, a tale to blend.
A warrior prince, in every part,

Abhimanyu, the young warrior, with a noble heart.

Thus, in echoes of honor, his story's sung,
Abhimanyu's valor, in verses strung.
A hero of heroes, forever young,
Abhimanyu's legacy, in epics hung.

1.23. Subhadra: The Radiant Princess

In the kingdom of Mathura, a princess fair,
Subhadra, with beauty beyond compare.
Sister of Lord Krishna, the divine and wise,
In the Mahabharata, her story lies.

A princess of grace, with a heart so pure,
Subhadra's virtues, forever endure.
In Dwarka's palace, her presence bright,
In every smile, she'd bring delight.

In the heart of Arjuna, she'd find her love,
Subhadra's union, blessed from above.
A wife so devoted, in every role,
In every joy, she'd play her role.

In the kingdom of Indraprastha, her home,
Subhadra's love, like a poem.
A mother of heroes, in every might,
In every battle, she'd stand in light.

In the end, her legacy, a tale of love,
Subhadra's devotion, in heavens above.
A princess of virtue, in every part,
Subhadra, the radiant princess, with a noble heart.

Thus, in echoes of honor, her story's sung,
Subhadra's love, in verses hung.
A princess of princesses, in love's lung,

Subhadra's legacy, in the songs of young.

1.24. Shikhandini: The Transformed Warrior

In the land of Panchala, a princess was born,
Shikhandini, with a fate forlorn.
Born as a girl, but a warrior at heart,
In the Mahabharata, her transformation a part.

Rejected by her father, for being not male,
Shikhandini's spirit, it did not fail.
With a resolve to change her fate's design,
In every battle, her courage would shine.

Seeking a boon to become a man,
Shikhandini's plea, a divine plan.
Transformed into Shikhandi, a warrior bold,
In every challenge, a story untold.

In the war of Kurukshetra, her role defined,
Shikhandi, with bow, her enemies she'd bind.
A key figure in Bhishma's fall,
In every arrow, she'd stand tall.

In the end, her fate, a victory won,
Shikhandi's battle, her story spun.
A warrior of courage, in every part,
Shikhandini, the transformed warrior, with a noble heart.

Thus, in echoes of honor, her story's sung,
Shikhandini's valor, in verses strung.
A warrior of warriors, in battles flung,

Shikhandini's legacy, in epics hung.

1.25. Eklavya: The Self-Taught Archer

In the forests of Hastinapura, a young boy grew,
Eklavya, with dreams anew.
Denied by a master, yet undeterred,
In the Mahabharata, his tale is stirred.

Belonging to a lower caste, he sought to learn,
Eklavya's passion, it did burn.
Crafting a statue of Drona, with devotion so true,
In every arrow, his skill grew.

Mastering the art of archery, on his own,
Eklavya's prowess, like seeds sown.
A self-taught archer, with talent rare,
In every shot, his dedication glare.

In the presence of Drona, he sought to train,
Eklavya's determination, a story plain.
Asked for his thumb, the price of his skill,
In every pain, he'd hold his will.

In the battlefield of life, his mark he'd leave,
Eklavya's story, in legends weave.
A symbol of perseverance, in every part,
Eklavya, the self-taught archer, with a noble heart.

Thus, in echoes of honor, his story's sung,
Eklavya's talent, in verses strung.
A hero of humility, forever young,

Eklavya's legacy, in epics hung.

1.26. Ghatotkacha: The Mighty Warrior

In the forests of Kamyaka, a hero was born,
Ghatotkacha, with strength to adorn.
Son of Bhima and Hidimba fair,
In the Mahabharata, his feats rare.

A warrior of might, with a heart so bold,
Ghatotkacha's prowess, in stories told.
In the Rakshasa clan, he'd shine bright,
In every battle, he'd take flight.

In the court of Indraprastha, his valor known,
Ghatotkacha's presence, like a cyclone.
A warrior prince, with powers grand,
In every challenge, he'd take his stand.

In the war of Kurukshetra, his role defined,
Ghatotkacha, with mace, his enemies bind.
His feats of bravery, in every fight,
A hero of the night, in honor's light.

In the end, his sacrifice, a hero's end,
Ghatotkacha's legacy, to the heavens ascend.
A warrior prince, in every part,
Ghatotkacha, the mighty warrior, with a noble heart.

Thus, in echoes of honor, his story's sung,
Ghatotkacha's valor, in verses strung.
A hero of heroes, forever young,

Ghatotkacha's legacy, in epics hung.

1.27. Barbarika: The Unstoppable Archer

In the land of the Yadavas, a prince was born,
Barbarika, with skills to adorn.
Son of Ghatotkacha and Maurvi fair,
In the Mahabharata, his prowess rare.

A warrior of speed, with a heart so bold,
Barbarika's archery, in tales unfold.
In the forests he trained, with determination true,
In every arrow, his skill grew.

Given the boon of three arrows by God,
Barbarika's power, like lightning rod.
A warrior unmatched, with weapons in hand,
In every battle, he'd take his stand.

In the battlefield of Kurukshetra, his might known,
Barbarika's arrows, like seeds sown.
Khatushyamji in present times, his name,
In every fight, his valor the same.

His prowess in war, in every fight,
A hero of speed, in honor's light.

In the end, his sacrifice, a warrior's end,
Barbarika's legacy, to the heavens ascend.
A warrior prince, in every part,
Barbarika, the unstoppable archer, with a noble heart.

Thus, in echoes of honor, his story's sung,
Barbarika's valor, in verses strung.
A hero of heroes, forever young,
Barbarika's legacy, in epics hung.

Section - 2

2. The Heart of the Epic: Krishna's Divine Bonds

2.1. Krishna and Arjuna: The Divine Bond

In the epic of Mahabharata, their tale is told,
Krishna and Arjuna, with destinies bold.
One, the Lord divine, with wisdom so deep,
The other, a warrior, whose vows he'd keep.

On the battlefield of Kurukshetra, they stood,
Krishna, the charioteer, his guidance so good.
Arjuna, the archer, with doubts in his heart,
In Krishna's words, he found his start.

"Perform your duty," Krishna did say,
To Arjuna, who was lost in dismay.
The Bhagavad Gita, their dialogue divine,
In every verse, their bond did shine.

Through the trials of life, they'd face,
Krishna and Arjuna, in every place.
In every triumph, in every strife,
Their bond of friendship, a beacon of life.

In the end, their legacy, a tale of yore,
Krishna and Arjuna, forevermore.
A friendship divine, in every part,
Krishna and Arjuna, never apart.

Thus, in echoes of honor, their story's sung,
Krishna and Arjuna, in verses strung.
A bond of friendship, forever young,

Krishna and Arjuna, their journey begun.

57

2.2. Krishna and Draupadi: A Divine Bond

In the heart of the Mahabharata's grandeur,
Lies a tale of friendship, both pure and sure.
Krishna, the lord, with his divine grace,
Draupadi, the queen, in her rightful place.

A bond forged in the fires of adversity,
Their story unfolds with unwavering solidarity.
In the halls of Hastinapura, a dice game unjust,
Krishna's presence, Draupadi's trust.

With her honor at stake, she called his name,
Krishna, her savior, in the face of shame.
His divine intervention, her strength and might,
In Krishna's friendship, she found her light.

In the forest of exile, their bond did grow,
Krishna's wisdom, Draupadi's sorrow did know.
In her laughter, in her tears,
Krishna was with her, calming her fears.

On the battlefield of Kurukshetra, side by side,
Krishna and Draupadi, with valor and pride.
His words of wisdom, her guiding light,
Together they fought, for what was right.

In the end, their legacy, a story divine,

Krishna and Draupadi, in every line.
A bond of friendship, in every heart,
Krishna and Draupadi, never to part.

Thus, in echoes of honor, their story's told,
A tale of friendship, timeless and bold.
Krishna and Draupadi, in eternity's hold,
Their bond of love, forever gold.

2.3. Krishna and Kunti: A Mother's Strength

In the annals of the Mahabharata's lore,
Lies a bond of love, so rich and pure.
Kunti, the queen, with a heart so kind,
Krishna, the lord, with wisdom refined.

A mother of valor, Kunti's tale unfolds,
Krishna, her guide, in life's manifold.
In her moments of joy, in her hours of woe,
Krishna's presence, a comforting glow.

In the exile's trials, Kunti found her might,
Krishna's counsel, her beacon of light.
In the palace's intrigues, in the war's demand,
Krishna and Kunti, hand in hand.

A bond of devotion, in every prayer,
Krishna, the divine, always there.
In her plea for guidance, in her silent cries,
Krishna's wisdom, a mother's eyes.

In the end, their legacy, a tale of love,
Kunti and Krishna, in heavens above.
A bond of kinship, in every part,
Krishna and Kunti, heart to heart.

Thus, in echoes of honor, their story's sung,
A mother's strength, with the divine One.

Krishna and Kunti, forever young,
Their bond of love, forever strung.

61

2.4. Krishna and Bhishma: The Warrior's Respect

In the battlefield of Kurukshetra, a warrior stood tall,
Bhishma, the grandsire, with honor's call.
Krishna, the charioteer, with a solemn vow,
To respect Bhishma, in battle's brow.

A warrior of ages, Bhishma's might,
Krishna's reverence, in every fight.
In the bed of arrows, his resolve firm,
In Krishna's eyes, his valor affirm.

In the court of Hastinapura, his word was law,
Bhishma's wisdom, like a flawless jaw.
Krishna's admiration, in every glance,
In Bhishma's valor, his respect enhance.

In the end, his sacrifice, a warrior's fate,
Bhishma's legacy, in Krishna's state.
A warrior of righteousness, in every part,
Bhishma, the grandsire, with a noble heart.

Thus, in echoes of honor, their story's sung,
Krishna and Bhishma, in verses strung.
A bond of respect, forever young,
Krishna and Bhishma, their journey begun.

2.5. Krishna and Karna: The Friendship Tested

In the annals of the Mahabharata's lore,
Lies a friendship, tested and pure.
Karna, the warrior, with a heart so kind,
Krishna, the charioteer, with wisdom defined.

A friendship forged in the fires of life,
Karna and Krishna, amidst strife.
In the face of adversity, their bond did grow,
In every trial, their friendship show.

Karna's loyalty, in every deed,
Krishna's friendship, in every need.
In the battle of Kurukshetra, their paths did cross,
In every arrow, their friendship emboss.

In the end, his fate, a warrior's end,
Karna's legacy, to the heavens ascend.
A friend of friends, in every part,
Karna, the warrior, with a noble heart.

Thus, in echoes of honor, their story's sung,
Krishna and Karna, in verses strung.
A bond of friendship, forever young,
Krishna and Karna, their journey begun.

2.6. Krishna and Shakuni: The Cunning Rivalry

In the game of dice, a rivalry did brew,
Shakuni, the mastermind, his plans askew.
Krishna, the strategist, with schemes so grand,
To counter Shakuni's every demand.

A rivalry born of deceit and ire,
Shakuni and Krishna, in cunning's mire.
In every move, in every ploy,
Their rivalry, a tale of coy.

Shakuni's dice, loaded with deceit,
Krishna's wisdom, his plans to beat.
In the game of life, their paths did clash,
In every gamble, their rivalry rash.

In the end, their fate, a tale of woe,
Shakuni's legacy, in treachery's flow.
A rivalry of minds, in every part,
Shakuni, the mastermind, with a cunning heart.

Thus, in echoes of rivalry, their story's sung,
Krishna and Shakuni, in verses strung.
A tale of cunning, forever young,
Krishna and Shakuni, their rivalry flung.

2.7. Krishna and Duryodhana: The Divine Confrontation

In the halls of Hastinapura, a prince did reign,
Duryodhana, with ambition's bane.
Krishna, the diplomat, with wisdom's lore,
To confront Duryodhana's every chore.

A confrontation of righteousness and might,
Duryodhana and Krishna, in every fight.
In the game of kingdoms, their rivalry grew,
In every challenge, their stance they drew.

Duryodhana's envy, in every glance,
Krishna's resolve, in every chance.
In the war of Kurukshetra, their paths did meet,
In every battle, their rivalry replete.

In the end, their fate, a kingdom's fall,
Duryodhana's legacy, in ambition's thrall.
A rivalry of kingdoms, in every part,
Duryodhana, the prince, with an ambitious heart.

Thus, in echoes of rivalry, their story's sung,
Krishna and Duryodhana, in verses strung.
A tale of ambition, forever young,
Krishna and Duryodhana, their rivalry sprung.

2.8. Krishna and Dhritarashtra: The Blind King's Counsel

In the court of the Kauravas, a king did preside,
Dhritarashtra, the blind, with fate as his guide.
Krishna, the advisor, with wisdom so clear,
To guide Dhritarashtra, in every fear.

A king blinded by love for his son,
Dhritarashtra and Krishna, their bond begun.
In every decision, in every decree,
Their counsel, a tale of loyalty.

Dhritarashtra's dilemma, in every choice,
Krishna's wisdom, his voice.
In the face of war, their bond did strain,
In every sorrow, their friendship wane.

In the end, his kingdom lost,
Dhritarashtra's legacy, at a cost.
A king misguided, in every part,
Dhritarashtra, the blind, with a broken heart.

Thus, in echoes of loyalty, their story's sung,
Krishna and Dhritarashtra, in verses strung.
A bond of counsel, forever young,
Krishna and Dhritarashtra, their friendship sprung.

2.9. Krishna and Vidura: The Voice of Reason

In the court of the Kuru clan, a voice was heard,
Vidura, the wise, with wisdom's word.
Krishna, the ally, with counsel so true,
To guide Vidura, in all he knew.

A voice of reason, in every debate,
Vidura and Krishna, in counsel great.
In the halls of Hastinapura, their presence felt,
In every decision, their wisdom dealt.

Vidura's loyalty, in every decree,
Krishna's friendship, his plea.
In the face of war, their bond did stand,
In every trial, their friendship grand.

In the end, his legacy, a voice of truth,
Vidura's wisdom, in every sooth.
A voice of reason, in every part,
Vidura, the wise, with a noble heart.

Thus, in echoes of wisdom, their story's sung,
Krishna and Vidura, in verses strung.
A bond of counsel, forever young,
Krishna and Vidura, their friendship sprung.

2.10. Krishna and Gandhari: The Mother's Grief

In the halls of the Kuru court, a mother wept,
Gandhari, the queen, her sorrow kept.
Krishna, the comforter, with solace's hand,
To ease Gandhari's grief, in every land.

A mother's sorrow, in every tear,
Gandhari and Krishna, in sorrow's fear.
In the aftermath of war, their paths did cross,
In every loss, their grief emboss.

Gandhari's lament, in every cry,
Krishna's presence, her sigh.
In the face of tragedy, their bond did grow,
In every sorrow, their friendship show.

In the end, her legacy, a mother's love,
Gandhari's grief, in heavens above.
A mother's sorrow, in every part,
Gandhari, the queen, with a grieving heart.

Thus, in echoes of grief, their story's sung,
Krishna and Gandhari, in verses strung.
A bond of solace, forever young,
Krishna and Gandhari, their grief begun.

Conclusion

As we reach the end of our poetic journey through the Mahabharata, we are left with a profound sense of awe and wonder at the timeless wisdom and eternal truths contained within this epic narrative. "Mahabharata: Tales in Verse" has been a labor of love, a tribute to the rich tapestry of characters and events that have captivated hearts and minds for millennia. Through the medium of poetry, we have sought to breathe new life into these ancient stories, to illuminate their relevance to our lives today, and to inspire a new generation to discover the beauty and depth of this timeless epic.

At the heart of the Mahabharata lies the enigmatic figure of Krishna, whose presence permeates every aspect of the narrative. As the charioteer to Arjuna, he imparts the timeless teachings of the Bhagavad Gita, offering guidance on duty, righteousness, and the nature of existence itself. Through our poems dedicated to Krishna, we have sought to capture the essence of his character – his wisdom, his compassion, his playfulness, and above all, his divinity.

But Krishna is not the only character to shine in the pages of the Mahabharata. Each character, from the mighty Pandavas to the cunning Kauravas, from the virtuous Draupadi to the wise Vidura, has a story to tell, a lesson to teach, and a legacy to leave behind. Through our poems, we have endeavored to give voice to these characters, to explore their motivations, their fears, and their triumphs, and to show that their struggles are not so different from our own.

As we reflect on the epic journey we have undertaken, we are reminded of the timeless themes that run through the Mahabharata – the eternal struggle between good and evil, the complex nature of human relationships, the inevitability of fate, and the power of redemption. These themes are not confined to the pages of an ancient epic but are woven into the fabric of our lives, guiding our actions, shaping our beliefs, and challenging us to be better, to do better, and to live better.

"Mahabharata: Tales in Verse" is more than just a book of poetry; it is a testament to the enduring power of storytelling, to the richness of Indian culture and mythology, and to the universality of the human experience. It is a book that invites readers to immerse themselves in a world of heroes and villains, of gods and mortals, and to discover in its pages a reflection of their own hopes, fears, and dreams.

As you close this book, may you carry with you the wisdom of the ages, the beauty of the verses, and the inspiration of the characters who have walked the path of dharma before us. May the tales of the Mahabharata continue to inspire, enlighten, and entertain for generations to come, and may its echoes of honor, betrayal, and destiny resonate in our hearts forevermore.

Thank you for joining us on this poetic odyssey. Until we meet again, may your lives be filled with the light of knowledge, the warmth of love, and the strength of righteousness. Jai Hind! Jai Bharat!

Authors Biography

Dr. Ankush Mahajan

Ankushmahajan7dec@gmail.com

(+91-9781987223)

ORCID – 0009-0005-7529-2057

Dr. Ankush Mahajan is a distinguished writer and scholar, known for his profound insights into literature and his unwavering commitment to academic excellence. With a Master's degree in English and Philosophy, he has delved deep into the intricate realms of language, thought, and critical analysis. His academic journey culminated in a Ph.D. in English, where his thesis on 'The impact of The Bhagavad Gita on Ralph Waldo Emerson with reference to the Bhasya of Sri Adi Shankaracharya and Sri Ramanujacharya' showcased his deep understanding and meticulous research.

Beyond his academic pursuits, Dr. Ankush Mahajan is a prolific writer, contributing numerous articles to 'The Tribune,' a prestigious English newspaper in India. His love for writing extends to the world of journalism, where he brings a unique perspective informed by his scholarly background. Dr. Ankush Mahajan's passion for literature is not confined to the written word; he also holds a postgraduate diploma in journalism and mass communication with distinction, adding to his diverse skill set.

Dr. Ankush Mahajan's expertise in translation, demonstrated by his postgraduate diploma in translation (Hindi-English), further highlights his versatility. His dedication to academic and literary pursuits is evident in the vast number of papers he has published in both national and international journals, particularly in Scopus-indexed publications.

In addition to his academic achievements, Dr. Mahajan is a keen blogger, using his platform to share his insights and engage with a wider audience. His current focus is on writing books that cater to the needs of academia, reflecting his commitment to knowledge dissemination and scholarly enrichment.

Dr. Ankush Mahajan stands as a beacon of intellectual curiosity and scholarly rigor. His work is not just about the exploration of literature and ideas but also about the empowerment of others through knowledge. Through his books, articles, and blog posts, he not only shares his expertise but also inspires readers to embark on their own intellectual journeys. Dr. Mahajan's dedication to his craft is matched only by his desire to make a meaningful contribution to academia. His passion for literature and language is not just a professional pursuit but a personal quest to understand the complexities of the human experience. In every word he writes, Dr. Mahajan's commitment to knowledge, truth, and enlightenment shines through, making him a truly exceptional writer and scholar.

Dr. Shiva Durga

Department of English, Institute of
Applied Sciences & Humanities
GLA University, Mathura, 281406
(UP)
Email: shiva.durga@gla.ac.in
shivadurgasmailbox@gmail.com
Cell#: +91-9897768037
Educational Qualification: M.A.,
M.Ed., PhD.

Dr. Shiva Durga an esteemed scholar and the Chapter Head of the English Language Teachers' Association of India, has left an indelible mark on language studies. With an impressive portfolio of 30 published research papers, 32 conference presentations, and the facilitation of conducting 25 workshops in reputed organizations, Her leadership extends to national platforms as the Chapter Head of ELTAI, where she plays a pivotal role in shaping discourse and practices in English language education.

Beyond her prolific research contributions, Dr. Shiva Durga has been awarded the best National Coordinator for UGC SWAYAM MOOC under the Ministry of HRD and Education. Her dedication to online education spans six years, focusing on the exploration of the "Nature of Language." In this capacity, Dr. Durga has proven to be a visionary, contributing significantly to the evolution of educational practices and ensuring access to quality language education for a diverse audience.